Bedtime!

Gwenyth Swain

First Avenue Editions/Minneapolis

To find out more about the pictures in this book, turn to page 22.
To find out more about sharing this book with children, turn to page 24.

The photographs in this book are reproduced with the permission of: © Trip/R. Chester, front cover; © Jack Ballard/Visuals Unlimited, Inc., back cover; © Dermot Tatlow/Panos Pictures, p. 1; © Jennie Woodcock/ Reflections Photolibrary/CORBIS, p. 3; © Earl & Nazima Kowall/CORBIS, p. 4; © Trip/H. Rogers, pp. 5, 15, 17; © Jeff Greenberg/Visuals Unlimited, Inc., p. 6; © Betty Press/Panos Pictures, p. 7; © Mark E. Gibson/Visuals Unlimited, Inc., p. 8; © Robert van der Hilst/CORBIS, p. 9; © Jodi Jacobson/ Peter Arnold, Inc., p. 10; © Trip/D. Houghton, p. 11; © Sean Sprague/Panos Pictures, p. 12; © Owen Franken/CORBIS, p. 13; © Jeremy Hartley/Panos Pictures, p. 14; © Alison Wright/CORBIS, p. 16; © Trip/S. Grant, p. 18; © Giacomo Pirozzi/Panos Pictures, p. 19; © Dean Chapman/Panos Pictures, p. 20; © Deutsch/Sprague/Panos Pictures, p. 21.

Copyright © 2002 by Gwenyth Swain

First Avenue Editions
An imprint of Lerner Publishing Group, Inc.
241 First Avenue North
Minneapolis, MN 55401 U.S.A.

Website address: www.lernerbooks.com

Library of Congress Cataloging-in-Publication Data

Swain, Gwenyth, 1961–
    Bedtime! / by Gwenyth Swain.
      p. cm. — (Small world)
    ISBN-13: 978–1–57505–162–8 (pbk. : alk. paper)
    ISBN-10: 1–57505–162–1 (pbk. : alk. paper)
    1. Bedtime—Juvenile literature. 2. Sleeping customs—Juvenile
literature. [1. Bedtime. 2. Sleep.] I. Title. II. Small world (Minneapolis,
Minn.)
HQ784.B43 S83 2002
306.4—dc21   2001000051

Manufactured in the United States of America
3 4 5 6 7 8 – JR – 13 12 11 10 09 08

How sleepy are you?

Do you feel like whining
and rubbing your eyes?

Have you been up so long,
you can't help but cry?

Take a nap in a lap.

Grab a spot on a cot.

Snooze on an airplane
up high in the air.

Sleepyheads can sleep
almost anywhere!

Do you get much rest
away from home?

Do you sleep best
when you're not alone?

Brush your teeth
before you hit the sheets.

Put on pajamas. Cover your feet.

Give thanks. Say good night.

Don't forget to turn out the light.

Dream up in a hammock.
Sleep down on the ground.

Find the warmest,
softest pillow around.

Tuck yourself in till you feel snug.

Ask someone for a goodnight hug.

Lie close, warm, and safe.

Bedtime is the best time,
anytime, anyplace!

More about the Pictures

Front cover: Big sister reads a bedtime story to her brother in England.

Back cover: A Korean boy naps during a boat trip.

Page 1: Some tiny spectators just can't stay awake during this Tibetan opera performance.

Page 3: A tired British baby rubs her eyes.

Page 4: A mother in India holds on to her sleepy son.

Page 5: Sometimes when we're tired all we can think to do is cry.

Page 6: A child takes a nap on her father's lap in Polk City, Florida.

Page 7: In Trinidad, Cuba, children at a day-care center lie on cots at nap time.

Page 8: A young girl snoozes while a jet whisks her through the air, traveling hundreds of miles per hour.

Page 9: In Kuqa, China, a little boy falls asleep in a carpet shop.

Page 10: Sometimes it's hard to get sleepy, especially during a pillow fight.

 *Page 11:* This girl sleeps best when she's cuddling her Siamese cat.

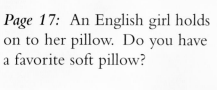 *Page 17:* An English girl holds on to her pillow. Do you have a favorite soft pillow?

 *Page 12:* In Prague in the Czech Republic, a boy brushes his teeth before bed.

 *Page 13:* A boy in Paris, France, sits snug in pajamas and looks at a book.

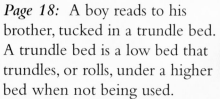 *Page 18:* A boy reads to his brother, tucked in a trundle bed. A trundle bed is a low bed that trundles, or rolls, under a higher bed when not being used.

 *Page 14:* It's bedtime for these children in Turkmenistan, a country in central Asia.

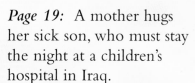 *Page 19:* A mother hugs her sick son, who must stay the night at a children's hospital in Iraq.

 Page 20: This young girl lies close to her mother in Thailand.

 Page 15: A girl in England reads on into the night, even after the lights are out!

 *Page 21:* Safe in a sling, this baby in Gautemala can sleep anytime, anyplace.

 *Page 16:* A baby in the Amazon River area of Peru rocks in a hammock.

A Note to Adults on Sharing This Book

Help your child become a lifelong reader. Read this book together, taking turns as you both read out loud. Look over the photographs and choose your favorites. Sound out new words and go back to them later for review. Then try these "extensions"—activities that extend the experience of reading and build discussion and problem-solving skills.

Talk about Bedtime

All around the world, people enjoy their rest. This book shows children asleep or getting ready for bed in many different countries and cultures. Ask your child to describe his or her bedtime routines. How do the bedtime routines shown in this book differ from those of your child? How are they the same?

Sleep in Different Ways

With your child, choose a new bedtime habit that you want to try. It can be as simple as singing a song or reading a story before going to bed. Or try these ideas: Borrow a hammock and try it out for a nap. Dig out a sleeping bag and have an indoor camping trip. Which way of sleeping seemed easier or harder? Warmer or cooler?